Single-context Words:
A Study of a Quirk of the English Language

Ian Yearsley

Published by Ian Yearsley

Publishing partner: Paragon Publishing, Rothersthorpe
First published 2020
© Ian Yearsley 2020

ISBN 978-1-78222-778-6

Book design, layout and production management by Into Print
www.intoprint.net
+44 (0)1604 832149

This book is dedicated to Rob Cumberland,
who shares my fascination for the oddities of language
and helped me identify several single-context words
and shape the rules for the genre

Introduction

This book is about what I call 'single-context words'. Such words, by my definition, are quite simply words which only ever appear in one context. A good example of this is the word 'aback', which is only ever used in the context 'taken aback'. The words around it can change – he was/they were/Steve was completely… etc. – but the word 'aback' itself is never used without the word 'taken' preceding it. That is the concept of a single-context word.

The first word that struck me as occurring in this way was 'aspersions' (they are always cast) and this realisation set me on a quest to find out if there were more words like it and, if so, why they should have survived. I enlisted the help of several people whom I either worked with or knew were interested in the use of language (or both) and between us we produced a list which I have since massively expanded into the content of this book.

As the words were being collected it became apparent that there were some patterns. Many of the words, sometimes termed 'fossil words', survive solely because they appear in a stock phrase or cliché – 'beauty is in the eye of the *beholder*', for example. Without such archaic survivals, the words themselves would probably not be in use at all.

Apart from words like 'aback' and 'aspersions' (which might be called 'hard' single-contexts), there are also some which are single-context, but which really feel like a bit of a cheat ('soft' single-contexts). These tend to be words which are followed by smaller parts of speech, e.g. 'appertaining' is always followed by 'to', 'devoid' is always followed by 'of'. These are single-context words – they just don't feel as 'right' as some of the others!

Apart from these definite single-context words, there are also several other categories which either are or aren't quite there. A 99% Rule has evolved to allow the inclusion of words which sound like they should be included, but which, in the strictest terms, probably should not be. The best examples of these are common nouns. 'Petard' (a type of cannon), for example, is only ever used in the phrase 'hoist by [one's] own petard'. Technically, however, it is possible to go to a museum of weaponry and say 'Hey - look at that petard!', but the phrase above is in such widespread use (and no other 'petard' phrase is) that it feels genuinely 99% single-context and therefore qualifies under my definition.

'Petard' is a near hit, but there are also some near misses. 'Compunction' and 'qualms' are good examples of this – nobody has any, but there is no single context. For example, 'He's got no qualms about...' and 'He doesn't have any qualms regarding...' are both possible versions. Other near misses include words like 'gallivant', which is usually followed by 'with', 'about' or 'around', so it is not a single-context word in strict terms, but it is used in roughly the same context on every occasion. 'Unwritten' is another example: it usually applies to laws, rules or codes, all of which are related senses, but there is no unique usage.

A further thing worth mentioning is the appropriateness of the different parts of speech to single-context words. There are eight main parts of speech:

- noun (a word used as a designation for a person, place, thing or idea, e.g. a table)
- pronoun (a word that can take the place of a noun, e.g. I, he, she or it)
- adjective (a word that describes a noun or pronoun, e.g. a **wooden** table)
- verb (a word used to describe an action or state of being, 'e.g. the dog barked')
- adverb (a word that describes the verb, e.g. 'the dog barked **loudly**')
- preposition (a word that describes the relationship between a noun/pronoun and something else, e.g. 'the cat sat **on** the mat')
- interjection (a word used to show excitement or exclamation, e.g. '**Wow**! That was amazing!') and
- conjunction (a joining word, e.g. 'the cat **and** the dog').

Single-context words appear quite commonly as nouns and adjectives, but not so commonly as prepositions or conjunctions. There are four main types of nouns: common nouns (i.e. physical things, such as a table), abstract nouns (i.e. concepts, such as anger), proper nouns (i.e. names, such as Liverpool) and compound nouns (nouns comprising more than one word, such as 'rearguard action'). I decided early on to leave out proper nouns, since these are names of people and places, which could be anything and are therefore effectively false, although an example is included in the appropriate section by way of illustration.

Finally, a word on hyphens. Where a word is hyphenated and the whole of that word is unique in its context (e.g. 'blue-arsed' fly) the word has been included. However, where only part of a hyphenated word is unique or both parts are unique but only within the whole word (e.g. 'fangled' in 'new-fangled' or 'hocus' and 'pocus' in 'hocus-pocus' respectively) the word has not been included, since the overall word is not unique.

I have relied heavily on the Oxford English Dictionary (OED, 'The definitive record of the English language': www.oed.com) for spellings, definitions and uses of words. It has helped me to rule some words in and some words out and to understand the subtleties of meaning and the historical contexts. Despite my above rules, and my attempts to remain fully objective, I have found it necessary on occasion to be flexible in ruling words in our out: on balance, I have used the weight or lack of evidence in the OED to justify inclusion or exclusion respectively. This book may not contain the full list and you may disagree with some of the more tenuous ones. I ruled some out during the writing up of my notes and added others in. All feedback and suggestions would be welcome via my website at www.ian-yearsley.com.

I hope this book is of interest to those who share my penchant for curious quirks of our rich and wonderful language. I would like particularly to thank Rob Cumberland for his help in compiling the original list and in helping me to determine some of the rules and definitions to go with this study of an unusual quirk of the English language.

Nouns

As mentioned in the Introduction there is a problem with single-context words which are nouns. There are fundamentally four types of noun:

a) Abstract nouns, which deal with concepts or ideas (anger, love, desire, etc.)

b) Common nouns, which describe physical things (table, chair, vehicle, etc.)

c) Proper nouns, which are the names of things (e.g. Dave, Essex, London, etc.)

d) Compound nouns, which are nouns comprising more than one word (e.g. 'hot dog' or 'attorney general').

Each of these comes with single-context issues, which are explored in the relevant section.

a) Abstract Nouns

Abstract nouns appear to provide some of the best examples of single-context words because, by their very nature, they are generally connected with thoughts and ideas rather than with tangible objects. They have consequently survived the test of time by being retained in otherwise out-dated snap phrases.

abeyance   **[in/into …]**

The word 'abeyance', which means 'the position of waiting for or temporarily being without', is always preceded by either the word 'in' or the word 'into', for example in the phrase 'the peerage has fallen into abeyance following the death of Lord Smith'.

aegis   **[under the … of]**

Originally from Greek mythology, 'aegis' was the shield of Zeus or Athene. Now it is used solely in the phrase 'under the aegis of' to mean 'under the protection or sponsorship of'.

aplomb   [with …]

The word 'aplomb', meaning 'self-possession', is always preceded by 'with', for example in the sentence 'he met the challenge with aplomb'.

ascendancy   [in the …]

'Ascendancy', meaning 'the state of being in the ascendant', is usually used in the phrase 'in the ascendancy', meaning 'on the rise', most commonly in the figurative context of a rising star or some movement in a sporting, musical, cinematic or political arena.

aspersions   [cast …]

The word 'aspersions', always used in the plural, incidentally, is only ever used in the phrase 'cast aspersions' to mean 'attack the reputation of'.

auspices   [under the … of]

'Auspices', meaning 'by the encouragement or sponsorship of', is these days almost always used both in the plural and in the phrase 'under the auspices of', i.e. 'in receipt of patronage' or 'under favourable influence'.

aversion   [… to]

The word 'aversion', which essentially means 'dislike', is almost always followed by the word 'to', for example in the phrase 'I have an aversion to spiders'.

bane   [… of (one's) life]

'Bane', which means 'ruin' or 'poison', is now in common usage only in the phrase 'bane of (one's) life', usually as a description of an annoying person or thing, i.e. someone who, or something which, is a constant and recurring irritant.

bee-line   [make a … for]

A 'bee-line' is technically a straight line between two points, such as a bee is supposed to use when returning to the hive. In practice, however, it is only ever used in the phrase to 'make a bee-line for', i.e.

head directly towards.

behest   **[at the ... of]**

The word 'behest', meaning 'command', is only ever used in the phrase 'at the behest of', for example 'at the behest of John' (or 'at John's behest') to mean 'at John's command'.

billy-oh   **[go like ...]**

The word 'billy-oh' (sometimes written 'billy-o') is used uniquely in the phrase 'go like billy-oh'. This phrase literally means 'like the devil' but is mostly used figuratively to imply speed and energy, e.g. 'your dog is running around like billy-oh', i.e. quickly and energetically.

caboodle   **[(the whole) (kit and) ...]**

A slang word, originally from America, 'caboodle' is used only in the related phrases 'the whole caboodle' or 'kit and caboodle', which is perhaps best summarised in single-context terms as '(the whole) (kit and) caboodle', meaning 'the whole lot of' or 'everything'. The OED states that it is 'supposed to be a corruption of the phrase *kit and boodle*', 'kit' in this sense being a kind of basket and 'boodle' being several things (e.g. people or animals) grouped together and 'considered collectively'.

chinwag   **[have a ...]**

'Chinwag' or 'chin-wag' is a slang word for a talk or a chat. It is most used in the phrase 'have a chinwag'.

climes   **[sunnier ...]**

The word 'climes', which is used to define a location which is generally identifiable by its climate, is nowadays generally only in widespread use in the phrase 'sunnier climes', and then invariably only poetically. An example would be 'Are you off to sunnier climes?', i.e. 'Are you going to a sunnier place?'.

codswallop   **[(a load of old) ...]**

Although the word 'codswallop', which is slang for 'nonsense' or 'drivel', can be used as an exclamation on its own (i.e. 'Codswallop!')

it is most commonly preceded by 'a load of old', as in, for example, 'What a load of old codswallop!', i.e. 'What a load of nonsense!'.

collywobbles   **[get/have the …]**

The OED defines collywobbles physically as 'a disordered state of the stomach characterized by rumbling in the intestines'. From thence it has passed into figurative use to mean 'a state of nervous fear'. It is usually used in the context of getting or having the collywobbles.

comeuppance   **[get one's …]**

Acknowledged by the OED to be used 'chiefly in "to get one's comeuppance"', this word means to receive a deserved punishment, e.g. 'the criminal ultimately got his comeuppance'.

cropper   **[come a …]**

The abstract noun 'cropper' is a slang word, originally meaning 'a heavy fall' but now used figuratively in the phrase to 'come a cropper', its only regular modern usage. There are three archaic common 'cropper' nouns for a type of pigeon, someone who raises crops and a small printing machine, but none of these is in widespread use today.

crux   **[… of (the matter/situation)]**

The word 'crux', meaning 'a point at issue', is always followed by 'of', usually in the phrase 'crux of (the matter/situation)', as, for example, in the following sentence: 'We need to get to the crux of the matter', i.e. 'we need to get to the real point which is at the heart of the discussion'.

dander   **[get (one's) … up]**

'Dander' has several meanings, including 'a piece of vitrified refuse of a smith's fire or furnace' and (in Scottish dialect) 'a stroll or saunter'. It is only in common usage, however, in the phrase 'to get (one's) dander up', i.e. 'to be in a ruffled or angry temper'.

daylights   **[the living …]**

Although the word 'daylight' (singular) has many contexts, the word 'daylights' (plural) is used almost exclusively in the phrase 'the living daylights' to mean 'with great severity or intensity', for example in the phrase 'it scared the living daylights out of her', i.e. it made her very, very scared. There are some variations on this phrase, but this is the one that is most heard. It is also the title of a James Bond film.

delectation   [for (one's) (delight and) ...]

The word 'delectation' means 'delight' or 'enjoyment'. It usually follows the word 'for' and is often also preceded by 'one's' (or variants of that) and even 'delight and', as in, for example, 'I have arranged some entertainment for your delight and delectation', meaning 'I have arranged some entertainment so that you've got something to enjoy'.

despond   [slough of ...]

'Despond', short for 'despondency', is an archaic word which is only ever used in the phrase 'slough of despond', meaning the act of being in despondency.

disservice   [do (somebody) a ...]

The word 'disservice', meaning 'the rendering of an ill service', is only ever used in the phrase 'do somebody a disservice', i.e. 'render them ill-service'. It is most used in the context of deliberately causing damage to a person's reputation through gossip or lies.

doldrums   [(down) in the ...]

The 'doldrums' is a region near the equator where the meeting of trade winds produces light, baffling winds, sudden storms and calms. Though usable in this context, it is more commonly found in general speech in the phrase '(down) in the doldrums' to mean 'depressed' or 'fed up', a usage which retains connections with the trade wind depressions of its origins.

dotage   [in (one's) ...]

'Dotage', which means 'impaired intellect, especially through old age', is only used in the phrase 'in (one's) dotage'.

drabs   [dribs and ...]

The word 'drabs' has several meanings, but its usage is now almost exclusive to the phrase 'dribs and drabs', i.e. 'in or by small intermittent amounts'. In this context it means a small or petty sum, usually of money. See 'dribs' below.

dribs   [... and drabs]

Initially meaning a small quantity of something, the word 'dribs' is now almost exclusively used in the phrase 'dribs and drabs', i.e. 'in or by small intermittent amounts'. See 'drabs' above.

dudgeon   [high ...]

'Dudgeon', which means 'resentment or feeling of offence', is only ever used in the phrase 'high dudgeon', as in for example 'he left the room in high dudgeon'.

durance   [in ... vile]

There are several obsolete meanings of the rarely heard word 'durance'. It survives in only one context, that of 'forced confinement' or 'imprisonment', especially in the phrase 'in durance vile', i.e. 'in unpleasant imprisonment'. The word has close associations with 'duress' (see below).

duress   [under ...]

The word 'duress' has several historic contexts (including 'confinement' – see 'durance' above), but the only common modern context is in the legal phrase 'under duress', which refers to 'constraint illegally exercised to force a person to perform some act', e.g. 'I forged the money under duress', i.e. against my will.

eeny, meeny, miny and moe

These four words are nonsense words which are used uniquely in a children's counting rhyme to select someone or something.

fettle   [in fine ...]

'Fettle', meaning 'condition' or 'trim', is only ever used in the phrase 'in fine fettle', for example in the sentence 'my recent lottery win has put me in fine fettle', i.e. made me feel in top condition.

figment [... of (one's) imagination]

The word 'figment', which means 'invented statement', is only ever used in the phrase 'figment of (one's) imagination'.

fount [... of all knowledge]

A 'fount' is a 'spring, source or fountain'. The word is in common use today only in the figurative phrase 'fount of all knowledge'. It was originally used poetically, but it now seems to be in wider usage and is often used ironically to refer to someone who thinks they know everything but doesn't.

fruition [come to ...]

The word 'fruition' can mean 'the action of enjoying' but it is most used in the phrase 'come to fruition' to mean 'bear fruit', e.g. 'his carefully thought out plan will come to fruition next week'. The OED notes that the word has been erroneously associated with 'fruit' but derives from an Old French word for 'enjoyment'.

fullness [in the ... of time]

Although the word 'fullness' does have other meanings it is used almost exclusively in the phrase 'in the fullness of time', i.e. in due course or eventually.

gab [gift of the ...]

'Gab', meaning 'talk', 'prattle', etc., is only ever used in the phrase 'gift of the gab' to mean 'a talent for speaking'.

gamut [(the) (whole) ... of]

A syntactically complex single-context word originating from musical notation, 'gamut' has a few variations on the words that can surround it, but its most regular usage is in the phrase '(the) (whole) gamut of', i.e. 'everything within the available range'.

gift-horse [(don't) look a ... in the mouth]

The word 'gift-horse' is only ever used in the phrase '(don't) look a gift-horse in the mouth'. This is an excellent example of a single-context word, with a long set-phrase around it. The word originates from the practice of giving a, presumably valuable, horse as a gift; it consequently refers to a gift or opportunity which is so freely given and so valuable that it is too good to turn down.

gist   **[get the … of]**

'Gist', which means 'real point or substance of the matter', is only commonly used in the phrase 'get the gist of', i.e. 'grasp the meaning of'.

groundswell   **[… of opinion]**

A 'groundswell' is a heavy sea-swell as the result of a distant storm, but in everyday language its only usage is in the phrase 'groundswell of opinion', used to signify growing popular feeling about a topical issue.

gunpoint   **[(held) at …]**

The word 'gunpoint' is only ever used in the phrase 'at gunpoint', often as '(held) at gunpoint' in the context of a kidnapping, when the kidnapper has hostages and a gun.

gusto   **[with …]**

'Gusto', meaning 'zest or enjoyment', is used only in the phrase 'with gusto', to signify the zest or enjoyment with which something is done.

gyp   **[give (someone) …]**

The word 'gyp' is a slang word, used only in the phrase to 'give (someone) gyp', i.e. to 'punish or treat someone roughly', frequently in a verbal context and in a teasing or jokingly critical manner.

habdabs   **[the screaming …]**

'Habdabs', sometimes corrupted to 'abdabs', means a nervous anxiety. It is usually preceded by the words 'the screaming', often in the context of a person being given 'the screaming habdabs', i.e. being made to feel extremely anxious by some occurrence that they perceive as unfortunate.

ides [(beware) the ... of March]

Famously referenced in William Shakespeare's play, *Julius Caesar*, 'ides' are a Roman measurement of date, occurring once a month. In practice, the word is only in general use in the Shakespearian phrase '(beware) the ides of March' (15th March), traditionally the day predicted for the murder of Caesar and hence an inauspicious day to be watched out for.

impunity [with ...]

'Impunity', meaning 'exemption from punishment, penalty, injury or loss', is always preceded by 'with'.

iniquity [den of ...]

The word 'iniquity', meaning 'wickedness', can in theory be used on its own, but in practice it usually follows the words 'den of', to refer to 'a wicked place'.

intents [to all ... and purposes]

The word 'intent' is used in many contexts, but the plural, 'intents', occurs in only one: the phrase 'to all intents and purposes', meaning 'for all practical purposes'.

juncture [at (this) ...]

A 'juncture', a place where things join, originated as a physical thing, but the word is now invariably used figuratively, especially in the phrase 'at (this) juncture', meaning 'at (this) point in time'.

ken [beyond our...]

'Ken' is a Scottish derivative word meaning 'range of sight or knowledge'. It is only ever used in general speech in the phrase 'beyond our ken' to mean 'outside what we know'.

kibosh [put the ... on]

The word 'kibosh' is a slang term found only in the phrase 'put the kibosh on', meaning 'put an end to, dispose of finally'.

kilter   [out of …]

'Kilter' (sometimes spelt 'kelter') is a word that means to be in good health or spirits. It tends only to be used in the phrase 'out of kilter', meaning 'out of sorts' or 'out of alignment'.

let   [… or hindrance]

The word 'let' has many meanings, but in one of its archaic senses of 'hindrance, stoppage or obstruction' it survives only in the phrase 'let or hindrance' to describe something that gets in the way or impedes progress.

limbo   [in …]

'Limbo' is an interesting word. It has two main modern meanings: 1) 'a region supposed to exist on the border of Hell as the abode of the just who died before Christ's coming, and of unbaptized infants'; and 2) 'a dance in which the dancer bends backwards and passes under a horizontal bar raised only a few inches off the ground'. Both uses describe states of being that are between one thing and another, leading to the common phrase 'in limbo', meaning 'between one thing and something else'. 'Limbo' is also 'a South African name for a coarse calico'.

loggerheads   [at …]

Although the word 'loggerhead' has other contexts, the plural, 'loggerheads', is used only in the phrase 'at loggerheads', meaning to disagree about something.

lucre   [filthy …]

'Lucre', which means 'gain', is now used only in the phrase 'filthy lucre' to mean 'dishonourable gain, often of money'.

meemies   [(have/get) the screaming …]

Originally meaning 'drunk or disorderly', the word 'meemie' has come to mean 'in a state of hysteria' and is now almost exclusively used in the phrase 'to have [or to get] the screaming meemies', i.e. to become hysterical. In the Second World War the phrase was used

as the name for a German rocket mortar which made a distinctive sound.

meeny – see 'eeny'

mickey [take the ... (out of)]

The word 'mickey' is an interesting one. It has several colloquial uses which mean different things in different English-speaking nations (i.e. it means different things in Australia, Canada and Ireland). In colloquial British usage it appears chiefly in the phrase 'take the mickey (out of)', i.e. 'make fun of, satirize, or debunk a person or thing'.

midst [in the ... of/in (someone or something's) ...]

'Midst', meaning 'middle', is a word that is regularly used in two phrases, but they are so similar that it just about qualifies as a single-context word. The phrases are 'in the midst of' and 'in (someone or something's) midst'. 'In ... midst' is therefore a clear central theme here.

miny – see 'eeny'

misadventure [death by ...]

The noun 'misadventure', meaning 'bad luck or misfortune', can be used on its own, but it is most commonly found in the legal phrase 'death by misadventure' to refer to some kind of 'fatal mishap' or a 'death caused accidentally'. There is also a verb 'to misadventure', but that is rarely used.

mock-holiday [play ... with]

The word 'mock-holiday' is not in common use. When it is used, it is used exclusively in the phrase 'to play mock-holiday with', meaning 'to deceive, make a mockery of, or take liberties with'. It is derived from the adjective/noun combination 'mock holiday', i.e. not a proper holiday.

mockers [put the ... on]

This plural word derives from the singular, 'mocker', meaning a person who mocks. If there is more than one mocker, then the word 'mockers' could be used in that context. In practice, however, the plural is solely used proverbially in the phrase 'to put the mockers on', meaning 'to thwart an enterprise or bring bad luck'.

modicum   **[a … of]**

The word 'modicum', meaning 'small quantity or portion', is only ever used in the phrase 'a modicum of'.

moe – see 'eeny'

muchness   **[much of a …]**

'Muchness' is an excellent example of a single-context word, being used only in the phrase 'much of a muchness' to mean 'very much alike'.

off-chance   **[on the …]**

The word 'off-chance', meaning a slight or remote possibility, is usually used in the phrase 'on the off-chance', although there are other variants such as 'what is the off-chance that (something might happen) …?'.

offing   **[in the …]**

'Offing' is only ever used in the phrase 'in the offing', meaning 'ready or likely to appear'. It would seem to originate in this sole surviving context from the use of the word 'offing' to mean 'the part of the visible sea distant from the shore'.

once-over   **[give (something) the …]**

The word 'once-over', meaning 'a single rapid survey or examination', occurs only in the phrase 'give (something) the once-over', i.e. to carry such a survey out.

oodles   **[… of]**

'Oodles' (always in the plural) means 'large or unlimited quantities'. It is always followed by 'of', as in, for example, 'we won't run out of chips today – we've still got oodles of them left!'.

parlance   [common …]

The word 'parlance', meaning 'way of speaking', seems only to be used nowadays in the phrase 'common parlance' to refer to 'a way of speaking using colloquial or generally accepted words'.

pecker   [keep (one's) … up]

'Pecker' has several meanings, but in its meaning of 'courage or resolution' it is used solely in the colloquial phrase of encouragement 'keep (one's) pecker up', i.e. 'remain cheerful and steadfast in the face of difficulty'.

penchant   [… for]

The word 'penchant', meaning 'inclination' or 'liking', is always followed by 'for', for example in the sentence 'I have a penchant for ice cream'.

quandary   [in a …]

'Quandary', meaning 'state of perplexity' or 'difficult dilemma', is always used in the phrase 'in a quandary', i.e. to be in such a situation.

quids   [… in]

The word 'quid' is in regular use in the context of money. Originating as a singular concept (one quid), it is now in widespread use in the plural sense as well (e.g. 40 quid, i.e. 40 times one quid (or £40)). The original plural, 'quids', is, however, regularly used now only in the phrase 'quids in', meaning 'in luck or profit' or 'well off for money'.

riddance   [good …]

Although the word 'riddance' can mean 'the act of getting rid of something', it is only widely used now in the exclamatory phrase 'good riddance' – an expression of relief at being free of an unwanted person or thing.

semblance   [some/no … of]

'Semblance', meaning 'resemblance' or 'likeness', is always followed by 'of' and usually preceded by 'some' or 'no', e.g. 'there should always be some semblance of order in a classroom'.

shebang   [the whole ...]

Of American slang origin, the word 'shebang', which can mean a business premises such as a tavern or a store, or even a dwelling place, is only ever regularly used in the phrase 'the whole shebang', i.e. 'the complete thing'.

shrift   [short ...]

'Shrift' is an archaic word meaning 'confession, penance or absolution'. It is now only used regularly in the phrase 'short shrift', to mean 'be dismissive of somebody or something', a sense which derives from its original meaning of 'the little time left between condemnation and punishment/execution'.

shtook   [in ...]

'Shtook', meaning 'trouble', is always preceded by the word 'in'.

sleight   [... of hand]

The word 'sleight', meaning craftiness or cunning, is only generally used today in the phrase 'sleight of hand', i.e. 'acute manual dexterity during the performance of some trick'. This phrase (which can also be hyphenated) can be used either literally or metaphorically.

spate   [... of]

The word 'spate' means a flood or sudden inundation of water. It has been taken into figurative use to mean a sudden outburst or an unusually large quantity. It is usually followed by the word 'of', as for example in the phrase 'there has been a spate of burglaries in the area of late'.

tarnation   [in ...]

The word 'tarnation' is an Americanism derived from 'damnation'. It can be used on its own but is most commonly found in archaic literature or films where a character uses the (often unfinished) phrase 'what (or where) in tarnation...?!' to enquire about something that has gone wrong or is not what they expected, e.g. 'Where in tarnation has my horse gone? I only left it alone for a moment!'.

tatters   [in ...]

A tatter is an irregularly torn piece of fabric. The word is generally used nowadays in the plural and in the figurative sense in the phrase 'in tatters' to mean something that has been torn to pieces, such as a person's reputation.

throes   [in the ... of]

The word 'throes', meaning 'violent pangs' or 'desperate struggle', is always used in the plural and only ever in the phrase 'in the throes of', i.e. to be suffering from these conditions.

tizzy   [in a ...]

'Tizzy', which was originally slang for 'dither', is only ever used in the phrase 'in a tizzy', meaning 'dithering' or 'in a state of unrest and confusion'.

tod   [on (one's) ...]

The word 'tod' has a variety of meanings, but its only common usage is in the phrase 'on (one's) tod', i.e. to be on one's own.

travesty   [a ... (of justice)]

'Travesty', meaning 'ridiculous', always follows the word 'a' and is often, though not always, followed by the phrase 'of justice'. It is usually used nowadays in an exclamation of contempt about the lack of application of justice, both in court cases and in more everyday situations, for example in the phrase 'that decision was a travesty of justice'.

tribulations   [trials and ...]

The word 'tribulations', meaning 'great affliction or misery', is only ever used in the phrase 'trials and tribulations', to imply major suffering. It is always used in the plural.

trice   [in a ...]

'Trice' has several meanings, but it is only widely used today in the phrase 'in a trice', meaning 'in an instant'.

troth   [plight one's …]

The word 'troth', meaning 'truth' or 'faith', is only ever used in the phrase 'plight one's troth', i.e. 'pledge one's truth or faith'.

turpitude   [moral …]

A rarely heard word meaning 'baseness, depravity or wickedness', 'turpitude' is now only widely used in the phrase 'moral turpitude', a phrase applied to a person or organisation of questionable morals.

umbrage   [take …]

'Umbrage', meaning 'a sense of slight or injury', is always used in the phrase 'take umbrage', i.e. feel that sense and make it evident.

uptake   [quick/slow on the …]

The word 'uptake' can occur in noun or verb formats. All the verb uses are either obsolete or in Scottish dialect. In its noun format the word is most used in the phrase 'quick (or slow) on the uptake' to describe the relative speed of a person's capacity for understanding.

vim   [… and vigour]

The word 'vim', meaning 'energy', is originally colloquial American. It is always used in the phrase 'vim and vigour', usually to describe someone who displays great energy.

whammy   [double …]

Although the word 'whammy' can be used in a limited number of other contexts, it is found regularly only in the phrase 'double whammy' to mean 'an intense or powerful look' or 'something intense, upsetting, [or] problematic'. It comes from the U.S. where it originally meant (colloquially) 'an evil influence or hex'.

whip-round   [have a …]

A 'whip-round' is an appeal, often impromptu, for contributions to a fund or worthy cause. It is always used with the verb 'to have', as in 'have a whip-round', i.e. make such a collection.

b) Common Nouns

As explained in the Introduction most common nouns should probably be ruled out if one is being purist about the single-context concept because it is easy to point to a common noun thing (a 'petard' for example) and say, 'There is a such-and-such'. However, for the reasons given in the Introduction, many of these qualify under the 99% Rule. Some of them are now used more widely as abstract nouns than as common nouns (e.g. 'tenterhooks').

band-wagon   **[(jump) on the ...]**

A 'band-wagon' is 'a large wagon capable of carrying the band in a procession'. Its use in political rallies has led to it passing from literal to figurative usage in the phrase 'on the band-wagon', meaning 'joining a popular cause that is likely to be successful'. The phrase is usually preceded by the verb 'to jump', but similar verbs such as 'to hop' or 'to climb' can also be used.

barge-pole   **[I wouldn't touch (X) with a ...]**

The word 'barge-pole', which describes 'a long pole with which a barge is propelled', is only ever used in general speech in the colloquial phrase 'I wouldn't touch (X) with a barge-pole', a figurative meaning which translates as 'I wouldn't go anywhere near X' or 'I refuse to have anything to do with X'. However, it is technically possible to locate and hold a barge-pole and say something like 'Look at this barge-pole'; as explained above, this is a common problem with single-context common nouns.

beholder   **[beauty is in the eye of the ...]**

A 'beholder' is someone who beholds or looks upon someone or something. The word is only ever used in the phrase 'beauty is in the eye of the beholder', i.e. beauty is subjective and not everyone rates it the same. Again, however, it is technically possible to point to someone who is beholding and say something different, though such usage in this case is extremely rare.

biddy   [old ...]

The word 'biddy' has several meanings, but it is almost always used today in the context of a contemptuous description of an old person, generally a woman, who is fussy about or insensitive to the activities of the young. It is always, in this context, preceded by 'old'. See also 'codger' and 'fogey'.

bread-line   [on the ...]

A 'bread-line' was originally literally a line of poor people queuing for bread or some other foodstuff which was given to them as charity. The word originated in America *c.*1900. It has passed into figurative usage in the phrase 'on the bread-line', which is used to describe someone who is poor and having trouble making ends meet. Variants such as 'close to the bread-line' and 'below the bread-line' also occur.

chattels   [goods and ...]

The word 'chattels' is used to describe property of every kind except real estate. It is a word that can be used on its own, but it survives mainly in the phrase 'goods and chattels', a phrase often heard in legal circles.

choosers   [beggars can't be ...]

'Choosers' are 'people who choose'. The word is only ever used in the phrase 'beggars can't be choosers', i.e. 'people who don't have many options can't afford to be selective'. Although technically it is possible to point to such choosers and say something different about them, it is extremely unlikely for the word to be used in such a context.

cleaver   [meat ...]

The verb 'to cleave' means 'to part or divide by a cutting blow'. A 'cleaver' is consequently a tool used in the performance of such an activity. The word is most used in the phrase 'meat cleaver' to refer to a cleaver for cutting meat. Technically a 'cleaver' is also a 'person who cleaves', and the word also applies to a type of archaeological tool. Both these contexts are comparatively rare, however.

codger   [old …]

As with 'biddy', the word 'codger' is almost always used today in the context of a contemptuous description of an old person, generally a man in this case, who is testy, crusty or fussy about, or insensitive to, the activities of the young. It is always, in this context, preceded by 'old'. See also 'biddy' and 'fogey'.

copy-book   [blot one's …]

A 'copy-book' is a book containing copies for learners to imitate. Though technically it is possible to locate and hold such a book, it is only regularly referred to in the figurative phrase 'blot one's copy-book', meaning 'make a mistake', 'get a black mark' or 'spoil one's record'.

cortege   [funeral …]

This is an interesting one. A 'cortege' is a procession of people. The word could be used in any context, but it is invariably used in the context of death, especially in the phrase 'funeral cortege' – a procession of people or vehicles following a coffin or hearse.

cranny   [nook and …]

The word 'cranny', meaning 'crevice', is generally only in widespread use in the phrase 'nook and cranny', which is mainly used to refer to every possible place that something that is lost might be found in. The phrase can also be used in the plural – i.e. 'nooks and crannies' – and there is a case for putting forward 'nook' as a single-context word as well, although that is in more general widespread usage on its own, so it has not been separately included in this list. 'Cranny' can also be used on its own, e.g. 'have a look in that cranny [small space] over there', but such usage is much rarer than it is for 'nook'.

craw   [stick in one's …]

A 'craw' is a 'pouch-like enlargement of the oesophagus or gullet in many birds'. Although it is technically possible to observe such a thing physically, the word tends most commonly to be used in the derivative figurative phrase 'stick in one's craw', meaning 'difficult to digest' and, by extrapolation, 'difficult to accept', for example in the phrase 'it really sticks in my craw that John got the promotion and I didn't'.

crick   **[… in the neck/back]**

A sudden stiffness or immobility of the back or neck is often described as a 'crick', as in the phrase 'I've got a crick in my neck', i.e. 'my neck is stiff'. There are other 'crick' nouns, whose meanings include a device for lifting heavy weights and a North American variant of 'creek', but the stiff-neck usage is by far the most common. See also the verbs section below.

curlies   **[get/have (somebody) by the short and …]**

The word 'curlies' is American slang for short hair. It is used exclusively in the phrase 'to get [or to have] (somebody) by the short and curlies'. In the literal sense this means 'to have hold of them by the hair', but in the more commonly used figurative sense it means 'to have backed them into a corner which they will find it difficult to get out of'.

dervish   **[whirling …]**

A 'dervish' is a Muslim friar who has taken vows of poverty and austerity. Some orders of dervishes practice wild dancing, from which practice the word is almost exclusively used now in the phrase 'whirling dervish', to mean someone who moves around at speed and apparently directionless.

dint   **[by … of]**

The common noun 'dint' means a 'stroke' or a 'blow'. Its use in that context is rare nowadays and it survives most commonly in the phrase 'by dint of', meaning 'by force of' or 'by means of'.

ditch-water   **[as dull as …]**

Although it is possible to view, fall into or pump out ditch-water, the only common modern use of the word is in the phrase 'as dull as ditch-water', to mean 'as dull as the stagnant, stale, or foul water which collects in a ditch'.

doghouse [in the …]

'Doghouse' can literally mean 'a house for a dog' (i.e. a kennel) or anything resembling such a thing, but it is used most commonly in the figurative phrase 'in the doghouse' to mean 'in disgrace' or 'out of favour', the suggestion being that the out-of-favour individual has been sent to live in the doghouse as a punishment. In jazz slang, the phrase 'a doghouse' is sometimes used for 'a double bass'.

droves [in …]

A 'drove' is a herd, flock, crowd or multitude, usually in a farming context. Today the word is only in regular everyday usage in the plural, and then only in the phrase 'in droves', for example in the sentence 'tourists visit London in droves', i.e. lots of them visit at the same time.

earshot [within/out of …]

The word 'earshot' has two contexts: 'within earshot' and 'out of earshot', 'earshot' being 'the distance within which a voice can be heard'. It is included in this list because the base unit (i.e. the distance) of earshot is the same in both cases.

flotsam [… and jetsam]

The words 'flotsam' and 'jetsam' (meaning 'floating wreckage on the sea' and 'items thrown overboard from a boat' respectively) can be used individually, but they are almost invariably used together in the phrase 'flotsam and jetsam' to refer to anything, particularly a jumble of items, found floating in the sea, however it got there.

fogey [old …]

As with 'biddy' and 'codger', the word 'fogey' is almost always used today in the context of a contemptuous description of an old person, generally a man but possibly of either sex, who is fussy about or insensitive to the activities of the young and possessed of antiquated ideas. It is always, in this context, preceded by 'old'. See also 'biddy' and 'codger'.

glimmer   **[... of (hope)]**

The word 'glimmer', which can mean 'a feeble or wavering light' or 'a tremulous play of reflected light', can be used on its own, but it is almost invariably followed by 'of'. In addition to that, the word is often used figuratively in the phrase 'glimmer of hope' to signify 'a faint gleam of hope when all else looks lost'.

gloaming   **[roaming in the ...]**

'Gloaming' is Old English for 'evening twilight'. It can still be used alone in that context, but that usage has become quite archaic. It consequently crops up regularly only in the phrase 'roaming in the gloaming' (meaning 'going for a walk in the twilight'), which is a line from, and the title of, a song by Sir Harry Lauder which was written in 1911.

Grail   **[Holy ...]**

'Grail' has various historical meanings, including 'gravel', 'a comb-maker's file' and 'fish'. It survives most commonly today, capitalised, in the phrase 'Holy Grail' – the platter used by Jesus at The Last Supper. The Holy Grail is lost, and many have tried to find it; this has led to the phrase being used to describe any kind of quest for a valuable artefact or possession.

grist   **[... to the mill]**

The word 'grist' has several meanings, but it has survived primarily in the phrase 'grist to the mill', meaning 'a source of profit or advantage'. The word unsurprisingly originates from milling, where 'grist' can be corn put into the grinding process or the actual act of grinding.

gunship   **[helicopter ...]**

The unhyphenated noun, 'gunship', is used exclusively in the phrase 'helicopter gunship' to refer to a heavily-armed helicopter. In hyphenated form it used to be used to describe ships with guns on them, but that usage is now rare as there are various classes of armoured ship in existence.

halfpennyworth [... of]

A 'halfpennyworth' – often contracted to 'ha'p'orth' and other variants – is an amount of any commodity which has a value of half a penny. As a halfpenny coin no longer exists in UK currency, the word is used nowadays to mean 'a small quantity'. It is always (in all its variants) followed by the word 'of'.

harbinger [... of (doom)]

A 'harbinger' is a person who goes ahead of a group to prepare the way and announce the group's approach. Although this word can be used in other contexts, it is almost invariably used in the figurative context of 'harbinger of doom' – a sign that something bad is coming.

honcho [head ...]

'Honcho' is an American word for a leader of a small group or squad. It is almost exclusively used in the tautological phrase 'head honcho'.

hustings [on the ...]

Almost always used in the plural, 'hustings' is a word that derives from the Anglo-Saxon for an assembly for the deliberation of a topic. Although it can be used more generally, it is usually found in the phrase 'on the hustings', meaning 'on the election trail'. A 'hustings' was, prior to the 1872 Ballot Act, a temporary platform from which election candidates were announced and made their opening speeches.

jetsam [flotsam and ...]

See 'flotsam'.

kith [... and kin]

Evolving from an original meaning of 'knowledge of a place with which one is familiar' to mean specifically country folk and kinsmen one knows in that locality, the word 'kith' is now exclusively used in the phrase 'kith and kin', an all-encompassing reference to an individual's relatives and family members.

lading   **[bill of …]**

A 'bill of lading' is 'an official detailed receipt given by the master of
a merchant vessel to the person consigning the goods, by which he
makes himself responsible for their safe delivery to the consignee'.
This document is 'the legal proof of ownership of the goods' and
'is often deposited with a creditor as security for money advanced'.
The word 'lading', which derives from the verb 'to lade', is a variant
of 'loading'. The act of lading consequently involves the loading
of cargo onto a ship. There also seems to be some cross-over with
'ladling', in which context 'lading' can be used to describe loading or
unloading a liquid into or out of a drinking vessel. The word exists
in other obsolete, archaic and little-used contexts, but 'bill of lading'
is its only common usage.

mainbrace   **[splice the …]**

'Mainbrace' is a nautical term describing 'the brace [a rope] attached
to the main yard [a wooden spar]' on a ship. As with other common
nouns it is possible to point one out, but the word is used almost
always these days in the phrase 'splice the mainbrace'. This was
originally a literal meaning – 'join the ends of two ropes together by
twisting and interweaving their individual strands' – but it has passed
into figurative use to mean 'serve an extra ration of rum' or, more
generally, 'start drinking' or 'drink freely'. This probably arose from
the practice of giving an extra tot of rum to sailors who physically
spliced the mainbrace.

nape   **[… of the neck]**

The word 'nape' has several meanings, one of which is 'the back of
the neck'. In this context the tautological phrase 'nape of the neck'
is almost exclusively used.

petard   **[hoist by one's own …]**

A 'petard' is a small bomb which can be used to blow a hole in a gate
or a wall by someone attacking a fortress. It is technically possible to
point to one, especially in a museum, and say 'look at that petard',

but the only common usage of the word today is in the phrase 'hoist by one's own petard' to mean 'blown up by one's own device'. This usage is applied figuratively rather than literally in most cases to mean 'undone by one's own machinations'. The word 'hoist' here is also interesting. It does not derive from the verb 'to hoist', the past tense of which would be 'hoisted', but from the verb 'to hoise', meaning 'to blow up', the past tense of which is 'hoised', corrupted to 'hoist'.

pillage   **[rape and ...]**

'Pillage', meaning 'the action of plundering or looting', can be used on its own, but it is usually used in the phrase 'rape and pillage', often in the context of an invading army wreaking damage and destruction on an invaded country's treasures.

purveyors   **[... of]**

The word 'purveyor', meaning 'a person who supplies or provides something', can be used on its own, but it is usually used in the phrase 'purveyor of', especially by individuals or organisations trying to signify high-class or quality provision of whatever it is that they purvey (supply).

rarebit   **[Welsh ...]**

'Rarebit' is 'a dish of melted and seasoned cheese on toast'. Although the word can be used on its own, it is most commonly found in the phrase 'Welsh rarebit', a cheese-on-toast dish which tends to have more ingredients, including for example butter, flour, mustard, beer, wine and various seasonings. The 'Welsh' element appears to derive from a period in the 17th and 18th centuries when all things Welsh were viewed as being of inferior quality, suggesting that it may have started life as a dish resorted to when meat was not available.

sackcloth   **[... and ashes]**

'Sackcloth' is a coarse textile fabric used for making sacks. While it is possible to refer to sackcloth alone, it is only commonly mentioned now in the phrase 'sackcloth and ashes', a phrase which means 'penitential garb'. Sackcloth is the roughest material out of which clothing would usually be made and it would therefore be something worn only by those doing penance. Ashes would be sprinkled on such a penitent's head as part of this act.

sandboy   [happy as a …]

A 'sandboy' is a boy who hawks sand for sale. The word is only ever used in the phrase 'happy as a sandboy'. It is unclear why sandboys should be particularly happy.

smithereens   [in/to …]

A 'smithereen' is a tiny fragment. The word is only really used in the plural now to refer to something that has been split into fragments, usually by a violent act or explosion. It is always preceded by 'in', 'to' or 'into', as in the phrase 'the ship was blown to smithereens'.

snook   [cock a … at]

The word 'snook' technically means the jokey, supposedly contemptuous gesture that one makes at another person by putting one's thumb on one's nose and spreading one's fingers out. Although the word has other meanings, it is now only widely used in the phrase 'cock a snook at' – originally meaning to make that gesture, now in more widespread figurative use to mean 'be contemptuous towards'.

squib   [damp …]

A 'squib' is an explosive device, usually used in the context of a firework. The only common usage of the word is in the phrase 'damp squib', a firework which failed to go off, or, figuratively, a plan which failed to realise its potential.

stead   [in (X)…]

The word 'stead', which usually refers to 'a place' of some kind, has many archaic and obsolete meanings. It also survives in words such as 'farmstead' and 'homestead'. When used on its own it tends now to follow the word 'in' in phrases such as 'in good stead', meaning 'to be in a good place', or 'in one's stead', meaning 'instead of'.

stickler   **[... for]**

'Stickler' has several meanings, but in the sense of 'a person who insists that something should follow a prescribed form or be done in a particular way' it is almost always followed by 'for' as in, for example, 'he is a stickler for following the Highway Code', i.e. 'he follows the Highway Code to the letter'.

tenterhooks   **[on ...]**

'Tenterhooks' were hooks used in the cloth industry to hook cloth onto a wooden frame (a 'tenter'). The attachment of the cloth to the hooks was a skilled job which had to be done correctly; if not, then the cloth could come off the hooks. The phrase 'on tenterhooks' arose from this activity to mean 'on edge' or 'in suspense'. Although it is possible to view tenters and tenterhooks, especially in museums, in practice the word 'tenter' has fallen out of use and the word 'tenterhooks' survives only in the phrase 'on tenterhooks'.

touchpaper   **[light the blue ...]**

'Touchpaper' is a paper used for lighting gunpowder. In practice though, the word is now used only figuratively and only in the phrase 'light the blue touchpaper', meaning to initiate a course of potentially dramatic events.

trove   **[treasure-...]**

The word 'trove' is an interesting one. It exists solely as the short form of the word 'treasure-trove', meaning 'a reserve or repository of valuable things'. That word is excluded from this list because it is never used in a unique sense. However, as the word 'trove' is used uniquely in this way, it ought to be included.

tuffet   **[Little Miss Muffet sat on a ...]**

A 'tuffet' is a hillock or grassy mound. Whilst it is technically possible to point out such a thing, the word is only really used in the nursery rhyme, 'Little Miss Muffet sat on a tuffet'.

war-path   [on the ...]

The word 'war-path' originates from North American Indian culture and was used to describe a literal path to war. It now survives only in the figurative context, 'on the war-path', meaning 'to be on the look-out for a fight or confrontation with a foe'.

wayside   [by the ...]

A 'wayside' is the side of a road or path, but the word is usually now used only figuratively and only in the phrase 'by the wayside', often preceded by 'fall' or 'go', to mean failing to stay the course or dropping out.

wildfire   [spread like ...]

A 'wildfire' (the word can be hyphenated as 'wild-fire') is a furious or destructive fire or conflagration, usually large-scale and outdoors, which can be difficult to extinguish. Whilst wildfires like this can be viewed in places such as California, which have a very dry climate, the word is in practice only used in the UK in the figurative phrase 'spread like wildfire', meaning to move rapidly and swiftly with devastating effect.

c) Proper Nouns

Proper nouns ought to be ruled out because, being names, they could be anything. There is, however, one which warrants inclusion.

Jove   [By ...]

The word 'Jove' is a poetic name for the planet Jupiter, but it is only used now in the exclamation 'By Jove!'.

d) Compound Nouns

alec/aleck   [smart ...]

Although 'Alec' is a Proper noun, and therefore inappropriate for inclusion in the above section because it is a name, the lower-case version, 'alec', is used in the compound noun 'smart alec' to mean 'someone who is, or wishes to appear to be, clever and knowing, but is widely regarded as smug and annoying'. The word sometimes has a 'k' on the end thus: 'smart aleck'. This compound noun is of North American colloquial origin.

bumpkin   [country ...]

A 'bumpkin' is 'an unsophisticated or socially awkward person from the country'. The word is frequently preceded by the unnecessary word 'country' in compound-noun form as 'country bumpkin'. The phrase is usually used derogatorily. A bumpkin is also a Scottish country dance and a barrel-like vessel used to carry water.

busman's   [... holiday]

A 'busman's holiday' is 'a holiday or other period of leisure time in which a person does something of a similar nature to his or her normal occupation'. It presumably derives from the once-common habit of a bus driver or bus conductor going on holiday by bus.

rearguard   [... action]

The word 'rearguard' has several solo uses, principally in military and sporting contexts, but in general use it is almost always used in the compound noun 'rearguard action' to mean 'the defensive action of a retreating army to fight off its pursuers'. The phrase is used figuratively more than literally these days.

runcible   [... spoon]

'Runcible' is a nonsense word invented by the 19th-century poet, Edward Lear, which has passed into common usage in the phrase 'runcible spoon' to describe 'a type of fork, curved like a spoon and typically having three broad prongs, one of which has a sharp edge'.

thermidor   [lobster ...]

'Thermidor' was the eleventh month of the French revolutionary calendar. It also means 'a moderate reaction following a revolution'. In practice, however, the word is used exclusively now in the compound noun 'lobster thermidor', a dish of 'cooked lobster mixed with a cream sauce, returned to its shell, sprinkled with cheese, and browned in the oven'.

unforced [... **error**]

Originating as a sporting term, the compound noun 'unforced error' means 'an error caused by one's own misjudgement, rather than by the skill of an opponent'. It has passed into more widespread use to refer to 'a careless or stupid error made when one is not under any particular pressure'.

vantage [... **point**]

The word 'vantage' has several solo uses, each derived from, and having some sense of, 'advantage'. In general usage it occurs most regularly in the compound noun 'vantage point', i.e. 'an advantageous viewing point'. It can be used in this context figuratively or literally.

Pronouns

There do not appear to be any pronouns which are single-context words.

Adjectives

An adjective is a descriptive word applied to a noun, e.g. a <u>black</u> cat or a <u>wooden</u> table.

addled   [... brain]

The adjective 'addled' is almost always used in the phrase 'addled brain' to mean 'muddled' or 'having lost the ability to think clearly'. It can, however, also be used to describe a rotten egg. The short-lived and non-functioning Parliament of 1614 was called 'the Addled Parliament'. The verb 'to addle' has several variations and meanings.

aforethought   [malice ...]

The word 'aforethought', meaning 'entertained in the mind beforehand' or 'premeditated', is most used in the legal phrase 'malice aforethought' to refer to a premeditated crime.

akimbo   [arms/legs ...]

Originally meaning 'with hands on hips and elbows turned outwards', the word 'akimbo' has also been adopted for use with legs. It is therefore usually found in two phrases – 'arms akimbo' (which is tautological) and 'legs akimbo'.

bare-faced   [... cheek]

The word 'bare-faced' (which is also available unhyphenated) originates from a physical description of a man without a beard. Its usage has expanded from that origin to mean 'without a mask' or 'undisguised', in both the literal and figurative senses. Although it can still be applied in such contexts, it is almost exclusively used now in the tautological phrase 'bare-faced cheek' to mean 'so undisguised that the person concerned does not care if they are behaving wrongly'.

bare-knuckle   [... fight]

The word 'bare-knuckle' is used solely in the context of a bare-knuckle fight – a fight without (boxing) gloves. It can be used figuratively as well as literally.

bated   **[with … breath]**

Although it has other archaic meanings as a verb, the word 'bated' in its adjectival form is used exclusively in the phrase 'with bated breath' to mean 'with breathing subdued or restrained under awe, terror or some other emotion'. It has associations with the word 'beat' in the latter's meaning of 'beat down' or 'put an end to'.

beady   **[… eye(s)]**

The word 'beady' means 'like a bead'. It is used exclusively in the context of 'beady eye(s)' (singular or plural). It can be used literally, but it is more likely to crop up in speech in a figurative sense to imply that a person is keeping a close watch on something or someone. It is frequently used as a warning, as in, for example, 'I've got my beady eye on you', to mean 'I'm watching you, so you'd better not misbehave'.

beholden   **[… to]**

The word 'beholden', meaning 'under personal or moral obligation', is usually followed by 'to', for example in the phrase 'she knew she would be beholden to him forever'.

bereft   **[… of]**

'Bereft' is an adjective meaning 'forcibly deprived'. It derives from the word 'bereave', as in 'bereavement', and is almost always followed by 'of', as for example in the sentence 'he was bereft of confidence as he had been lied to before'.

blithering   **[… idiot]**

Deriving from the verb 'to blither', which means 'to talk nonsense', the word 'blithering' is used only in the phrase 'blithering idiot' to describe a person who talks nonsense.

blood-curdling   **[… scream]**

The word 'blood-curdling', meaning 'very frightening' or 'spine-chilling', is almost always used in the phrase 'blood-curdling scream', especially in the contexts of crime or horror.

blue-arsed   [like a … fly]

The word 'blue-arsed' is only ever used in the phrase 'like a blue-arsed fly', to mean 'engaged in constant, frantic activity'. The word is comparatively modern and derives from the bluebottle, a dark-blue blowfly.

bounden   [… duty]

Deriving from the word 'bound', 'bounden' is almost exclusively used in the phrase 'bounden duty', meaning 'under obligation' or 'indebted to'.

break-neck   [… speed]

'Break-neck' is a word used to describe the likelihood of one breaking one's neck or, more generally, endangering one's life. Historically, it has been used in the context of dangerous places like cliffs and bends, but it is almost always used now in the phrase 'break-neck speed' to mean 'a dangerous speed at which to travel'.

browned   [… off]

The word 'browned' means 'to become brown'. It can be used in the context of colour changes, but it is almost invariably used now in the phrase 'browned off', i.e. to be bored or fed-up. The origin of the word in this context is unclear. See also 'cheesed' below.

builded   [And was Jerusalem … here]

'Builded' is an archaic, poetic word meaning 'built'. It is no longer in common usage but has survived because it features in a poem called 'Jerusalem' by William Blake (1757-1827) which has been set to music by Sir Hubert Parry (1848-1918) and is performed annually as part of the Last Night of the Proms celebrations at the Royal Albert Hall. The relevant words, which refer to an alleged visit of Jesus Christ to England, are as follows: 'And was Jerusalem builded here/Among these dark satanic mills?'.

callow   [… youth]

The word 'callow', which literally means 'immature' or 'inexperienced', can be used in several contexts, but its most common usage is in the phrase 'callow youth' to describe an immature or inexperienced youngster. It also features in the context of 'callow down' to describe the down of a fledgling bird or the soft facial hair of a boy.

catslide   [... roof]

A 'catslide roof' is a sloping roof on a building which continues below the main eaves almost to the ground. Its design allows for the building to have greater depth without increasing its height. The word 'catslide' is not used in any other context. The name presumably derives from the likelihood of a cat sliding off it.

cheesed   [... off]

'Cheesed off' is a phrase which means 'fed up' or 'annoyed'. Its origin is uncertain, but one now rare meaning of the word 'cheese' is 'discontinue' or 'leave off'. This is possibly a corruption of the word 'cease', so 'ceased off' might have been a more appropriate phrase to pass into the language. See also 'browned' above.

circumstantial   [... evidence]

Although the word 'circumstantial' can be used in several contexts, it survives most commonly in the legal phrase 'circumstantial evidence' to mean 'indirect evidence inferred from circumstances which afford a certain presumption or appear explainable only on one hypothesis'. 'Circumstantial' itself means 'relating to or dependent upon circumstances'. The word also has some largely archaic uses as a noun.

civvies   [in one's ...]

'Civvies' is a corruption of 'civilian clothes'. It tends to be used most frequently during wartime, especially in the context of 'in one's civvies' to describe a person who has left, or is leaving, the armed forces to wear civilian clothes. See also 'civvy' below.

civvy   [... street]

The word 'civvy' is a corruption of civilian. As with 'civvies' (see above), it tends to be used most frequently during wartime, to distinguish civilians from individuals serving in the armed forces. The word occurs only in the phrase 'civvy street', which is especially used in the context of a serviceman or -woman returning to normal, civilian life.

cruciate   [... ligament]

The word 'cruciate' means 'in the shape of a cross'. Whilst many things can be described as cruciate in that general sense, the word tends to be used most in the phrase 'cruciate ligament', of which there are two in a knee joint which cross over one another.

cursory   [... glance]

The phrase 'cursory glance' means to 'run the eyes quickly over something so as not to take in the details'. The word 'cursory' can be used in other contexts, but the sense in modern usage is almost always a visual one (including, for example, 'cursory inspection', 'cursory view', etc.).

deathless   [... prose]

The word 'deathless' has several senses but in one sense it is used exclusively in the phrase 'deathless prose', usually by critics in the often-ironic context of 'never to be forgotten' (and not necessarily for the right reasons).

demob   [... happy]

'Demob' is short for 'demobilisation', a word which is used most in the context of the First and Second World Wars for service personnel who are being discharged from duty and allowed to return to normal, civilian life. Such individuals were understandably elated to be going home because of their release from military service. The derived phrase, 'demob happy', is used to describe anyone who is deliriously excited or elated because of impending release from a job, assignment or posting. Technically, phrases such as 'demob suit' or 'demob leave' are permissible, but these have retained their specific wartime connotations and have not passed into general, everyday usage.

desiccated   [… coconut]

The verb 'to desiccate' means 'to dry' or 'to deprive of moisture'. Whilst this action could be taken in respect of many commodities, it is only commonly used in the adjectival phrase 'desiccated coconut', to describe coconut that has been dried to preserve it for later use, usually in cooking.

devoid   [… of]

The word 'devoid' is always followed by 'of' to mean entirely lacking in some attribute or another, e.g. 'he was devoid of charisma'.

diaphanous   [… gown]

The adjective 'diaphanous', meaning 'transparent', could be used to describe anything with that quality, but in practice it is used most in the phrase 'diaphanous gown', to describe a see-through or partly see-through dress.

double-edged   [… sword]

Originally used in several contexts, 'doubled-edged' is now only really used in the phrase 'double-edged sword'. Literally this means having two cutting edges. Figuratively it is applied to all situations where a benefit has been identified which may simultaneously have a disbenefit attached to it, suggesting that the potential benefit owner needs to exercise caution before proceeding to claim it.

dulcet   [… tones]

'Dulcet', meaning 'sweet', is in regular use these days only in the phrase 'dulcet tones', to describe a sweet sound, usually someone's voice, and often in an ironic or familiar context.

extenuating   [… circumstances]

The word 'extenuating' is used chiefly in the phrase 'extenuating circumstances', which means 'circumstances that tend to diminish culpability', e.g. 'It wasn't entirely my fault; there were extenuating circumstances'. See also 'mitigating' below.

fine-tooth   [… comb]

Although the hyphenated word 'fine-tooth' can be used to describe the thin, closely set teeth of a file or a saw, it is most widely used in the phrase 'fine-tooth comb' to suggest paying close attention to, and carefully sifting, evidence, as in 'I went through it with a fine-tooth comb but still couldn't find anything'.

foregone [… conclusion]

Literally meaning something that has previously happened, the word 'foregone' is only regularly used today in the phrase 'foregone conclusion', to mean an outcome that is known before all the factors relating to it have been considered, e.g. 'the planning application for the new road will be passed even if the consultation results come down against it; it's a foregone conclusion because the Council wants to build it anyway'.

foreseeable [… future]

The word 'foreseeable' means 'that may be foreseen'. It is used chiefly in the phrase 'foreseeable future'.

gainful [… employment]

'Gainful', meaning 'leading to [usually] financial gain', is used mainly in the phrase 'gainful employment', often in the context of an individual who has eschewed such activity in preference to being idle, e.g. 'he needs to find some gainful employment to keep him off the streets and out of trouble'.

go-faster [… stripes]

This hyphenated word is attributed to something, usually a vehicle, whose appearance has been modified in some usually superficial way to suggest that it can go faster than it can. The iconic use of the word is in the phrase 'go-faster stripes', signifying design stripes on the side of a car which suggest that the vehicle is capable of high speed or at least has a sporty appearance. The phrase is used ironically, often critically, with the implied suggestion that the stripes make the vehicle more appealing while simultaneously not adding any benefit to its function.

graven   [... image]

Literally meaning 'engraved' or 'sculptured', the word 'graven' is used most frequently in the phrase 'graven image' to describe a carved representation of a god which is used during worship.

greenfield   [... site]

The phrase 'greenfield site', which has only come into popular usage since around the turn of the century, literally means a site that has never been built on. The word 'greenfield' can, however, also be used on its own in the context of a newly identified business opportunity.

halcyon   [... days]

A halcyon was a fabled bird which bred around the time of the winter solstice in a nest floating on the sea. It could charm the wind and waves to keep the sea calm during its breeding season of around fourteen days. This bird is usually identified as a type of kingfisher, as that belongs to the scientific genus, *halcyon*. 'Halcyon days', by interpolation, are therefore calm and quiet days, which are often fondly remembered.

hale   [... and hearty]

There are lots of meanings to the word 'hale', but in adjectival use it has the single specific meaning of 'free from injury' or 'safe and sound'. It is only commonly used in the phrase 'hale and hearty', meaning 'free from infirmity' or 'sound in constitution'.

hang-dog   [... expression]

A 'hang-dog' (noun) was a low or unpleasant person who was fit only to hang a dog or to be hanged like one. This noun is now obsolete, but the word has survived adjectivally in the phrase 'hang-dog expression' to mean 'characteristic of a hang-dog', i.e. someone who has a base or degraded look about them.

hard-earned   [... cash]

The word 'hard-earned' is uniquely used now with 'cash' to signify a financial reward that has been earned through hard work.

headless   **[...chicken]**

Whilst almost anything that should have a head but doesn't could be described as 'headless', by far the most common usage of the word in practice is in the figurative phrase 'headless chicken', meaning 'disorganised and panicky, usually when doing more than one thing at a time'.

heinous   **[... crime]**

'Heinous', meaning 'hateful' or 'wicked', can be used in different phrases, but it is used chiefly to characterise crimes or those who commit them. It consequently appears most frequently in the stock phrase 'heinous crime', which is used to describe particularly despicable criminal acts.

hemmed   **[... in]**

The adjective 'hemmed' is used almost exclusively in the phrase 'hemmed in', meaning 'trapped, confined or imprisoned'. The term derives from sewing, in which context it relates to garments which are sewn with a hem. Such garments could easily be described as 'hemmed', but that is a very specific sewing context.

het   **[... up]**

'Het' is a corruption of 'heated'. It is used almost exclusively in the phrase 'het up' to mean 'in a hot temper'.

high-sided   **[... vehicle]**

The word 'high-sided' could be used to describe anything with high sides, but in practice it is used most commonly in weather reports during windy conditions when measures such as closing exposed bridges to 'high-sided vehicles' (to stop them blowing over) have been taken.

hobnail   **[... boot]**

A 'hobnail' (noun) is a short nail with a large head. Whilst it is possible to view or hold a hobnail, the word tends mostly to be used adjectivally in the phrase 'hobnail boot'.

horseless   [... carriage]

Although 'horseless' – literally meaning 'without a horse' – is a description that could be applied to several scenarios, the word is almost exclusively used in the phrase 'horseless carriage', a literal description of early motor vehicles which was in common usage *c.*1895-1910 and is still used in a nostalgic or slightly ironic/humorous sense.

ilk   [of this/that ...]

The word 'ilk' means 'the same'. It is chiefly used in the phrases 'of this ilk' and 'of that ilk' to mean 'just like this' and 'just like that' respectively.

ill-gotten   [... gains]

The phrase 'ill-gotten gains' means 'material goods or benefits that have been gained by evil means'. 'Gotten' is the obsolete past participle of 'get'. That word is still used in that context in America, but not usually in the UK.

immemorial   [since time ...]

Literally meaning 'beyond memory', the word 'immemorial' is used almost exclusively in the phrase 'since time immemorial' to mean 'a long, long time ago' or even 'since the beginning of time'.

inalienable   [... rights]

The word 'inalienable', which means 'cannot be transferred from its present ownership', is usually found in the phrase 'inalienable rights'. The word can be used on its own, but the context is almost always to do with property or possessions.

incarnate   [devil ...]

The adjective 'incarnate', meaning 'in human form', can be used alone but it is most found in the phrase 'devil incarnate', i.e. 'devil in human form'. The OED notes that this phrase is 'applied hyperbolically to a person, the true meaning is often more or less lost sight of'. There is a verb, 'to incarnate', which means 'to embody in flesh'.

inclement   **[... weather]**

'Inclement', meaning 'extreme' or 'severe', is used only in the context of weather, especially cold or stormy weather.

incontrovertible   **[... evidence]**

The word 'incontrovertible' means 'incontestable' or 'indisputable'. Whilst such a description could be applied to many things, in practice the word is used almost exclusively in the phrase 'incontrovertible evidence' to mean 'evidence which is so convincing that it cannot be disputed'.

kindred   **[... spirit]**

The word 'kindred', which was originally used to describe relationships by blood or marriage, has several uses, but it is only in common usage in the phrase 'kindred spirit', meaning 'to be of the same opinion or behaviours as someone else', e.g. 'I think I have found a kindred spirit', i.e. someone who thinks and acts like me.

knee-jerk   **[... reaction]**

Although the physical jerking of a knee could be referred to as a 'knee-jerk', especially in a medical context relating to nerve testing, the word is only really used figuratively in the phrase 'knee-jerk reaction' to mean 'an automatic or instinctive reaction whose consequences have not been fully thought through'.

madding   **[... crowd]**

An archaic word meaning 'becoming mad' or 'maddening', 'madding' has secured iconic status in the phrase 'madding crowd' in two literary contexts: firstly, in Thomas Gray's 1751 poem, 'Elegy in a Country Churchyard' ('Far from the madding crowd's ignoble strife'); and secondly, as a direct result of that, in the title of Thomas Hardy's 1874 novel, 'Far From The Madding Crowd'. In both literary works it means 'away from the madness of busy places' and it has passed into general usage in that context.

mitigating   **[... circumstances]**

'Mitigating', meaning 'alleviating' or 'extenuating' (see above), is frequently used in the (often legal) phrase 'mitigating circumstances' to mean a situation which lessens culpability and therefore permits a more lenient punishment.

mulled   **[... wine]**

According to the OED there are 17 uses of the word 'mull': 11 as nouns; six as verbs. The word 'mulled' is a unique adjectival use which occurs in the phrase 'mulled wine', i.e. 'wine made into a hot drink with added, sugar, spices and/or fruit'. It can also be used to describe beer and/or cider which has been similarly treated. The derivation is from one of the six verbs 'to mull', which means 'to warm wine or beer'. See also 'mull' in the transitive verbs section.

neap   **[... tide]**

Used exclusively in the phrase 'neap tide', the word 'neap' is described by the OED as 'designating or relating to a tide occurring just after the first or third quarters of the moon, when the high-water level is lowest and there is least difference between high- and low-water levels'.

nth   **[... degree]**

Originating from the study of mathematics, the word 'nth' has passed into more general usage in the phrase 'to the nth degree' to mean 'to any extent' or 'limitless'.

olden   **[in ... days]**

The word 'olden' is used chiefly in the phrase 'in olden days' (sometimes 'in olden times'), meaning 'belonging to a past age'. The phrase has passed into popular culture thanks in part to Cole Porter's 1934 musical 'Anything Goes', whose title song contains the lines 'In olden days, a glimpse of stocking / Was looked on as something shocking / But now, God knows, / Anything goes'.

opposable   **[... thumbs]**

Although the word 'opposable' can be used in the context of

contradictions and opposites, it tends most commonly to be used in the phrase 'opposable thumbs', to describe the thumb of a primate (like humans) which can be placed 'to face and touch another digit' (finger). Opposable thumbs are often cited as one of the factors which led to humans becoming the dominant species on the planet.

out-of-court   [... settlement]

The hyphenated adjective 'out-of-court' is used almost exclusively a) in media reporting and b) in the phrase 'out-of-court settlement' to refer to a settlement between parties which has been or was going to go to court but which has been settled outside of court jurisdiction.

parlous   [in a ... state]

The word 'parlous', a corruption of 'perilous', has several meanings, but most are now obsolete. The usual sense now is in the phrase 'in a parlous state' to mean 'in a desperate or hazardous situation'.

prodigal   [... son]

'Prodigal', meaning recklessly wasteful, can be used in several contexts, but it is principally used in the phrase 'prodigal son' to describe a male heir who has lived a reckless or extravagant life away from home and has made a repentant return after wasting a fortune.

raring   [... to go]

The word 'raring', which derives from the verb 'to rear', meaning 'to rise up', is found most in the phrase 'raring to go'. Literally originally meaning 'rising in readiness' (e.g. on the hind legs, like a horse might), it is now used mostly figuratively to described someone who, or something that, is eager, keen and ready for immediate action.

red-handed   [caught ...]

The word 'red-handed' derives literally from a description of someone having blood on their hands after a murder and has been extended into figurative use almost exclusively in the phrase 'caught red-handed', meaning 'still bearing the obvious evidence of guilt'. There are 'red-handed monkeys' and 'red-handed tamarins' in zoology, but these are specific terms which are not in everyday use.

rife [(to be) …]

'Rife', meaning 'prevalent' or 'widespread', has many possible contextual uses, but in all of them it is always preceded by the verb 'to be', as in, for example, 'conspiracies are rife' or 'dissension was rife'.

rose-tinted [… spectacles]

Whilst various items can be tinted with the colour of rose, the phrase 'rose-tinted' is usually used in the figurative context of 'rose-tinted spectacles' to mean 'to look at something through generous, idealistic or forgiving eyes'.

roughshod [ride … over]

The word 'roughshod' is used to describe horses which have been badly shod, i.e. whose horseshoes have their nail heads projecting. It has passed from this usage into the figurative phrase 'to ride roughshod over', meaning to 'domineer or tyrannise over' or 'to treat without consideration'.

sawn-off [… shotgun]

The adjective 'sawn-off' (sometimes 'sawed-off') is exclusively used in the context of a 'sawn-off shotgun' to describe a shotgun which has had part of the barrel sawn-off to make it shorter and more lethal. Traditional shotguns can be manufactured with shorter barrels, but the term is still used for such guns even if no sawing off has taken place.

sceptred [… isle]

A sceptre is 'an ornamental rod or wand borne in the hand as a symbol of regal or imperial authority'. The word 'sceptred', which therefore means 'furnished with a sceptre' and consequently 'invested with regal authority', only regularly occurs in the phrase 'sceptred isle'. This phrase was used in William Shakespeare's *c.*1595 play, *Richard II*, and in the title of a 1990s radio series, and later a book, by the historian Christopher Lee about the making of the British people. It tends to imply fondness and nostalgia for the island of Great Britain. See also 'furnish' in the Verbs section.

scot-free   **[get off/go ...]**

The word 'scot-free', meaning 'without being punished', is most found in the phrases 'get off scot-free' or 'go scot-free', usually in the context of someone being let off a misdemeanour or escaping from some predicament without harm. 'Scot-free' can also mean 'without paying scot' (a tax or tribute paid by a feudal tenant to their lord or ruler, or to a bailiff or sheriff) but this meaning is archaic and therefore rarely used now.

scudding   **[... clouds]**

The word 'scudding' has many dialect meanings, especially in Scotland. It is, however, mostly used in practice to describe clouds which 'move briskly or hurriedly'.

self-fulfilling   **[... prophecy]**

According to the OED the word 'self-fulfilling' relates to an opinion or prediction and means 'giving rise to actions that bring about its fulfilment' or 'bound to be proved correct or come true because of conditions created by its being expressed'. Logically, many things could therefore be self-fulfilled, but the word tends to be used chiefly in the phrase 'self-fulling prophecy' to mean 'a prophecy which will come true as a result of its being expressed'. An example would be the panic-buying of wine which causes a wine shortage after predictions have been made that wine will soon run out.

self-made   **[... man/woman]**

The adjective 'self-made' is usually used in the phrase 'self-made man' and, increasingly, 'self-made woman', to describe someone who has achieved wealth or status through personal effort and/or hard work.

serrated   **[... edge]**

Although various items can be described as 'serrated', in practice the only common use of the word is in the phrase 'serrated edge', particularly in the forensic context of a knife used as a murder weapon. 'Serrated' means 'having a row of small, teeth-like projections'.

shell-like   **[… ear]**

The word 'shell-like', meaning 'like a shell', can be used to describe anything which fits that description, but it tends to be used in the phrase 'shell-like ear'. It is often used without the noun in that phrase, e.g. 'can I have a word in your shell-like?'.

shitless   **[scared …]**

'Scared shitless', meaning 'extremely scared' – or, literally, so scared that you could shit yourself – is the only modern phrase in which the word 'shitless' is used.

slap-up   **[… meal]**

The word 'slap-up' is used almost exclusively in the phrase 'slap-up meal' to describe a meal of superior quality or style.

soft-shoe   **[… shuffle]**

Whilst the word 'soft-shoe' can be used in several dance contexts, it is most used in the phrase 'soft-shoe shuffle' to describe a style of dance influenced by African-American traditions and performed by black-faced minstrels using nimble footwork.

spick   **[… and span]**

'Spick' can be used as a noun in several contexts, but as an adjective it is used exclusively in the phrase 'spick and span', meaning 'neat' or 'smart'.

tantamount   **[… to]**

The only current use of the word 'tantamount' is in the phrase 'tantamount to', which means 'amounts to the same thing' or 'equivalent to'.

thankless   **[… task]**

The word 'thankless', meaning 'not moved by, or expressing,

gratitude', can be used on its own, but it tends to be used mostly in the phrase 'thankless task' to describe a task for which one will get no thanks.

three-line   [... whip]

'Three-line whip' is a political term used to describe 'a written notice, underlined three times to indicate great urgency, requesting the attendance of members of Parliament at a particular parliamentary session'. It has passed into more general usage to mean any meeting or practice which it is mandatory to attend or comply with. It indicates that all other engagements should be put aside. A whip in this context is a member of a political party whose duty it is to secure the attendance of members of that party at important votes.

transcendental   [... meditation]

The word 'transcendental' has several uses, but it appears most usually in the phrase 'transcendental meditation', which, according to the OED, is 'a method of relaxation and meditation based on the theory and practice of yoga popularised in the West by the Maharishi Mahesh Yogi'. 'Transcendental' here means 'beyond the limits of ordinary experience'.

trenchant   [... views]

Whilst the word 'trenchant' has a range of uses, it tends to occur most commonly in the phrase 'trenchant views', meaning 'clear, incisive and effective'.

two-horse   [... race]

The adjective 'two-horse' is used only in the context of a 'two-horse race', i.e. a race in which only two of the contestants are likely winners.

ulterior   [... motive]

The word 'ulterior', meaning 'lying beyond that which is immediate or present', can be used in several contexts, but it is almost exclusively used in the phrase 'ulterior motive', to mean 'a motive which is not currently known to anyone other than the person who possesses it'.

unassailable   [… lead]

Often used in a sporting context, the adjective 'unassailable' most commonly appears in the phrase 'unassailable lead' to describe a team (or individual) which is so far ahead in a match or competition that it is highly unlikely to be caught.

unbowed   [bloody/bloodied but …]

'Unbowed' means 'not bowed or bent'. It has a couple of archaic uses but is usually encountered now in the phrase 'bloodied (sometimes bloody) but unbowed' to describe someone who has either literally come through a fight but remains standing or, more commonly figuratively, someone who remains resolute despite suffering adversity.

uncharted   [… waters]

The word 'uncharted', meaning 'of which there is not a map or a chart', is almost exclusively used these days in the phrase 'uncharted waters'. As most of the world has now been charted, it tends to be used more in the figurative than the literal sense.

undivided   [… attention]

Various things can be 'undivided', i.e. 'not broken up into parts', but in practice the word is used mainly in the figurative phrase 'undivided attention' to mean 'attention that is fully focussed on the topic in hand', e.g. 'he gave me his undivided attention', meaning 'he paid me his full attention and was not distracted by anything else'.

ungodly   [… hour]

Literally meaning 'not fearing or revering God' and therefore, by interpolation, 'wicked', the word 'ungodly' is mostly used now in the phrase 'ungodly hour' to mean 'extremely late in the day (or very early in the morning)', the implication being that this is causing annoyance to a third party, e.g. by the playing of loud music at midnight.

unleavened   [… bread]

'Unleavened', meaning 'made without yeast or any other raising agent', is almost always used in the phrase 'unleavened bread'. It can be used figuratively to mean 'not moderated by a modifying element', for example in the context of 'unleavened sadness', but this is rare.

unprovoked   [... attack]

Although 'unprovoked' can be used in other contexts, it is usually used today in the phrase 'unprovoked attack', i.e. an attack that was not provoked and appeared to lack a cause or motive.

unrequited   [... love]

The word 'unrequited', meaning 'not reciprocated', can be used in contexts such as 'unrewarded' or 'unavenged', but it is almost exclusively used in the phrase 'unrequited love', i.e. in the context of a person having a feeling of love towards someone else where that love is not reciprocated.

unsung   [... hero]

The word 'unsung' means 'not uttered by singing'. It is most used in the phrase 'unsung hero' to mean 'a hero whose achievements have not been recognised or celebrated', presumably not even in song, something which was once conventional practice.

unturned   [leave no stone ...]

Literally meaning 'not turned over', the word 'unturned' can be used to refer to anything in that state, but it is almost exclusively used now in the figurative phrase 'leave no stone unturned', i.e. 'search comprehensively for something (including, presumably, by turning over stones to see what lies beneath them)'.

varicose   [... vein(s)]

'Varicose' means 'swollen'. The only context it is commonly used in is in the phrase 'varicose veins', meaning 'swollen veins'.

vestal   [... virgin(s)]

A 'vestal virgin' was a chaste priestess who had charge of a sacred fire in the temple of Vesta near Ancient Rome. Although the word 'vestal', meaning 'pertaining to Vesta' (a Roman goddess), can be used on its own, its very specific contextual origin means that that would be highly unusual.

white-knuckle   [... ride]

Although it has other meanings in North America, the word 'white-knuckle', which originated there, is usually used in the UK in the phrase 'white-knuckle ride', a literal description of one's knuckles turning white because one is gripping so tightly in a fairground ride or other mode of transport which is proceeding scarily fast.

wishful   [... thinking]

'Wishful', meaning something that is 'desired' or 'longed for', is almost exclusively used in a modern sense in the phrase 'wishful thinking', to mean a 'belief or expectation, that is influenced by one's wishes to the extent that relevant (consciously) known facts are (subconsciously) ignored or distorted'.

wuthering   [... heights]

Known from Emily Bronte's 1847 novel, 'Wuthering Heights', the word 'wuthering' is described in the book as 'a significant provincial adjective, descriptive of the atmospheric tumult to which its [the building of the title] station is exposed, in stormy weather'. The word can be used on its own, but rarely is.

yore   [days of ...]

'Yore', meaning 'a time long ago', is only ever used now in the phrase 'days of yore', often in a nostalgic or romantic way.

Verbs

There are two types of verb: transitive and intransitive. A transitive verb must be used with an object, for example the verb 'to admire': it must be specified what is admired, e.g. 'he admired her courage'. An intransitive verb, on the other hand, does not need an object, e.g. 'to sneeze', as in 'he sneezed'; it is possible to sneeze without specifying an object.

Some verbs, for example the verb 'to jump', can be used in either sense, e.g. 'I jumped' (with no object, intransitive) and 'I jumped the fence' (with an object, transitive).

a) Transitive Verbs

abet   **[aid and ...]**

The transitive verb 'to abet' means 'to encourage or assist someone'. It can be used on its own, but it is usually used in the phrase 'aid and abet', often in the context of encouraging or assisting someone to do something wrong or even carry out a crime.

behoves   **[it ... (somebody)]**

The verb 'to behove' has several meanings, many of which are obsolete. It is usually used in a modern context in the phrase 'it behoves (somebody) to do (something)', e.g. 'it behoves him to tread warily', meaning 'it is incumbent upon or necessary for him to tread warily'.

bide   **[... one's time]**

Although the verb 'to bide' has other meanings, it is uniquely used in one of its transitive senses in the phrase 'to bide one's time', i.e. 'to await one's opportunity'.

blurt   **[... out]**

In its transitive use, the verb 'to blurt' is usually used in the phrase 'blurt out' to mean 'utter abruptly and impulsively'. It also has unconnected, mostly archaic, intransitive uses.

boggle/boggles   [... the mind/the mind ...]

Originating from the word 'bogle' – a spectre which was said to startle horses – the verb 'to boggle' is now almost always used in the phrase 'boggle the mind' to mean 'bewilder or astound'. The reverse phrase, 'the mind boggles', is also in widespread use 'to express the perceived difficulty of grasping a concept'.

broach   [... the subject]

'Broach' has several historical meanings but, as the OED acknowledges, the use of it in the phrase 'broach the subject', meaning 'begin to raise a topic for discussion', is its 'chief current sense'.

brunt   [bear/feel the ... of]

The word 'brunt', meaning 'the chief stress or shock of an attack', is most used in the phrase 'bear the brunt of', though it is possible to use it on its own.

champing   [... at the bit]

The verb 'to champ' means 'to crush or chew by vigorous action of the jaws' or 'to bite anything hard'. It is usually used in the context of a horse biting impatiently at the 'bit' (part of a harness). The phrase 'champing at the bit' has passed into figurative use to mean 'restlessly impatient to do something, especially in the face of a constraint'.

chivvy   [... (someone) along]

The word 'chivvy' is usually used in the context of 'chivvy (someone) along'. i.e. hurry them up a bit. It comes from the verb 'to chivvy', which means 'to harass' or 'to worry', like a dog might worry sheep. There is an unconnected, infrequently used verb of the same construct which means 'to knife'. The word 'chivvy' also exists in noun form, where it means 'face'. Neither of these latter two uses is now common.

crick   [... one's neck/back]

'To crick one's neck' (or back) means 'to twist or strain one's neck (or back), causing painful stiffness'. There are other meanings of 'crick', but in transitive verb form this one is unique. See the nouns section above for more information.

dandle   **[... on one's knee]**

The verb 'to dandle' means 'to move lightly up and down in the arms or on the knee'. It is usually used in the context of dandling a child on one's knee, i.e. having them sit on one's knee and moving them up and down in a playful fashion.

doff   **[... one's hat]**

'Doff', meaning 'take off' or 'remove', is almost always used in the context of 'doff one's hat', i.e. 'remove one's hat temporarily as a mark of respect or acknowledgement'.

extol   **[... the virtues of]**

The transitive verb 'to extol' has several obsolete uses but survives in only one sense: 'to praise highly'. It is almost always used in the phrase 'extol the virtues of', as in, for example, 'financial experts extol the virtues of that investment', i.e. it's a good one.

forfend   **[Heaven ... !]**

Rare in modern usage, the verb 'to forfend' means 'to forbid'. It is most used in the phrase 'Heaven forfend!' to mean 'God forbid (that such a thing might happen)!'.

furnish   **[... with]**

The word 'furnish' is an interesting one. It has some obsolete meanings and it can occur in phrases such as 'furnish forth', 'furnish out' and 'furnish up', but in practice it is found most commonly now in the phrase 'furnish with', a transitive verb sense which means 'provide or supply with something necessary or useful'.

gird   **[... one's loins]**

The verb 'to gird' means 'to surround oneself with a belt or girdle, especially for the purpose of tightening clothing to allow freer movement'. Its meaning originates in the literal sense, but the word 'gird' survives most commonly today in the sense 'gird one's loins', i.e. 'brace oneself for action', presumably having secured any loose clothing in the process.

gnash   **[… one's teeth]**

The word 'gnash' appears in three formats: as a verb; a noun; and an adjective. In every case, however, it relates only to teeth. It means 'to grind the teeth together in rage or anguish'. Its most common usage is as a verb, which is why it is listed in this section.

mended   **[least said soonest …]**

According to the OED there are 11 'to mend' verbs. One of these means 'to make amends or reparation for' or 'to atone for (a misdeed, an injury)'. In this sense this verb is now found 'only in the proverb *least said soonest mended*, which means 'the less said the better, as things will sort themselves out more quickly that way'. See also 'soonest' in the adverbs section below.

mete   **[… out]**

The word 'mete' has several obsolete uses. In transitive verb form it survives mainly today in the phrase 'mete out', meaning 'to allot in proportion', e.g. by determining and delivering an appropriate level of punishment for a crime.

mull   **[… over]**

According to the OED there are 17 uses of the word 'mull': 11 as nouns; six as verbs. The most common verb usage is in the phrase 'mull over', meaning 'ponder upon'. See also 'mulled' in the adjectives section.

outstay   **[… one's welcome]**

The word 'outstay' is almost always used in the phrase 'outstay one's welcome', meaning 'stay longer than the expected or permitted time'.

over-egg   **[… the pudding]**

Originating from baking terminology, the word 'over-egg' is used in the phrase 'over-egg the pudding'. Literally this means putting too much egg into a pudding, but it is in more common usage figuratively to mean 'go too far in exaggerating or embellishing something', thus causing the thing described to lose its importance or validity.

overstep   [... the mark]

Literally meaning 'to go beyond a socially acceptable or feasible limit', the verb 'to overstep' is usually used in the tautological phrase 'overstep the mark' (sometimes 'overstep the line'). This suggests that the person doing the overstepping ought to be aware of the line they are crossing.

raze   [... to the ground]

The verb 'to raze' has several different meanings, but most are either obsolete or rare. The only common modern usage is in the phrase 'raze to the ground', i.e. 'tear down, demolish or level a building'. It sounds counter-intuitive, because the similar-sounding verb, 'to raise', can be used to mean exactly the opposite, but the two are unconnected.

redouble   [... one's efforts]

In the sense of 'increase or multiply', the word 'redouble' is used regularly only in the phrase 'redouble one's efforts', meaning 'increase or intensify one's efforts', i.e. try even harder.

regale   [... with]

The verb 'to regale', meaning 'to please, treat or delight someone with some agreeable activity', has obsolete and rare intransitive uses, but in transitive form it is chiefly followed in its various constructs by the word 'with', as for example in 'the old colonel regaled the troops with tales of his adventures' or 'he regaled himself with a culinary treat'.

slake   [... one's thirst]

The verb 'slake' has many meanings, but most are obsolete or rare. One meaning is 'to hydrate'; another is 'to appease, allay or satisfy'. It is in almost a combination of these two senses that the word survives in its only common modern usage: 'slake one's thirst', i.e. 'satisfy one's thirst by taking a drink'.

stap   **[… my vitals]**

In verb usage the word 'stap' occurs exclusively in the phrase 'stap my vitals'. 'Stap' is a corruption of 'stop', but that is irrelevant really, as the phrase is used as an exclamation of surprise or anger, e.g. 'Stap my vitals! I thought you were dead!'. There is a rarely used noun, 'stap', which means 'a stave of a tub or a cask'.

wend   **[… one's way]**

The verb 'to wend' has many rare and obsolete uses. Its most common modern usage is in the phrase 'wend one's way', meaning 'proceed in an unhurried manner or by an indirect route'.

whet   **[… one's appetite/whistle]**

The verb 'to whet' has several archaic meanings, almost all to do with sharpening a blade or a point. From this comes the figurative derivation of sharpening (i.e. rendering more keenly) one's appetite or curiosity. The word is now used almost exclusively in the stock phrases 'whet one's appetite' or 'whet one's whistle'. The latter is more literal, meaning to take a drink; the former harks back to sharpening one's keenness to commence something.

wreak   **[… havoc/revenge]**

Another word with many obsolete uses, 'wreak' is found most in the phrase 'wreak havoc' or, sometime, 'wreak revenge'. It means 'to cause harm or damage, often by way of punishment or revenge'.

b) Intransitive Verbs

appertain   **[… to]**

All parts of the intransitive verb 'to appertain' are almost always followed by the word 'to', e.g. 'the troops appertaining to the nation', i.e. the troops belonging to the nation.

atone   **[… for]**

All parts of the intransitive verb, 'to atone' are almost always followed by the word 'for', e.g. 'you need to atone for your error', i.e. you need to make amends for your error.

augur   **[does not … well]**

Whilst other parts of the verb 'to augur' can be used in various phrases, the word 'augur' itself seems to be used only in the phrase 'does not augur well', i.e. 'some likely ill-consequence is sure to follow'.

betide   **[woe …]**

Like other words in the verbs section, 'betide' has other historical uses, but it is now almost exclusively used in the phrase 'woe betide', as in 'be on the look-out for any ill-fortune that follows the taking of a certain course of action'.

bode   **[does not … well]**

Very similar in use and meaning to 'augur' (see above), and with similar varied usage for other parts of the verb, the word 'bode' seems to be used only in the phrase 'does not bode well', i.e. 'things are likely to take a turn for the worst'.

deign   **[… to]**

All parts of the intransitive verb 'to deign' are almost always followed by the word 'to', e.g. 'the dog would not deign to bark at anyone', i.e. the dog would not think it worthy of itself to bother to bark at anyone. In an obsolete transitive sense, the verb meant the opposite of disdain (dis-deign).

eff   **[… and blind]**

The verb 'to eff' is used primarily in the context of 'effing and blinding', i.e. 'swearing profusely, using strong expletives'. 'Eff' (from the letter 'f') is shorthand for the swearword 'fuck'. It can also be used in the related phrase 'eff off', i.e. 'fuck off' (go away).

eke   **[… out]**

'Eke' exists in noun, adverb, transitive verb and intransitive verb formats, though some of its uses in these contexts are archaic or obsolete. In intransitive verb form it is used exclusively now in the phrase 'eke out', meaning 'make last the required time by good economical practice', e.g. 'I will just about eke out my last few pennies before I have to return home'.

faff   [… about/around]

The verb 'to faff' means 'to fuss' or 'to dither'. It is almost always followed by 'about' or 'around', e.g. 'I do wish you would stop faffing about!'.

fizzle   [… out]

Originally meaning 'to break wind without making a sound', the word 'fizzle' is now almost exclusively used in the phrase 'fizzle out', meaning 'to end in a feeble way'.

gad   [… about]

The word 'gad' is invariably followed by 'about' to mean 'wander or rove aimlessly, usually in search of pleasure'. There are other meanings of the word, but none is now in such common usage as this.

hunker   [… down]

According to the OED, the verb 'to hunker' means 'to squat, with the haunches, knees, and ankles acutely bent, so as to bring the hams near the heels, and throw the whole weight upon the fore part of the feet'. The various parts of the verb are almost always followed these days by the word 'down', as in for example 'we just need to hunker down and ride out the storm'. Although the origins of the meaning are literal, the verb is widely used in a figurative sense, especially in the military context of digging in to lie low for a period.

militate   [… against]

Whilst it is possible to use the word 'militate' in positive phrases such as 'militate for' or 'militate in favour of', it tends to be used most in the negative phrase 'militate against'. The basic word means 'to campaign' or 'to advocate a particular course of action'; in 'militate against' it means 'to be a powerful or conclusive factor against some conclusion or result' as, for example, in the phrase 'the high radioactivity of the material militates against its widespread usage'.

scrimp   **[… and save]**

The intransitive verb 'to scrimp' is often, though not always, followed in its various parts by the phrase 'and save', e.g. 'we used to scrimp and save', meaning 'we used to be careful with our money and have to economise'.

sidle   **[… up]**

The verb 'to sidle', meaning 'to move sideways or obliquely, often in a furtive or conspicuous manner', has several modern uses but it is invariably followed by the word 'up', as in, for example, 'he sidled up to her'.

Adverbs

An adverb is a descriptive word applied to a verb, e.g. in the phrases 'he drove <u>quickly</u>' or 'she turned <u>abruptly</u>'.

aback   [taken ...]

Meaning 'in a backward direction' or 'towards the rear', the adverb 'aback' can be used in a variety of contexts but is usually found only in the figurative phrase 'taken aback', meaning 'surprised, shocked or discomfited'.

afield   [far/further ...]

The word 'afield', meaning 'away from home', is usually used in the phrases 'far afield' or 'further afield', sometimes literally, sometimes figuratively, to mean 'a long way from home' or 'at a considerable distance'.

amok   [run ...]

'Amok', meaning 'in a frenzied way', is almost exclusively used in the phrase 'run amok', i.e. 'run around in a frenzy', with the implication being that damage or carnage may ensue.

askance   [look ... at]

The word 'askance', which means 'obliquely' or 'sideways', is used chiefly in the contexts of seeing or observing, especially in the phrase 'look askance at', i.e. 'observe something from the corner of one's eye, often surreptitiously'.

aweigh   [anchors ...]

The word 'aweigh' is used exclusively in the nautical context of 'anchors aweigh', an instruction given to sailors to raise the anchors on a ship. The derivation is probably from 'weight', as in taking the weight off the anchors by raising them.

diametrically   [... opposed]

The adverb 'diametrically' literally means 'in the manner or direction of a diameter' or 'along the diameter'. Its most common modern usage is figurative, usually in the phrase 'diametrically opposed', which is used to describe standpoints which are completely opposite to one another. Proponents and opponents of Brexit might be described as 'diametrically opposed in their views', for example.

doggo   **[lie/play ...]**

'Doggo', meaning 'lie flat, remain hidden' or 'lie quietly', is used only in the related phrases 'lie doggo' or 'play doggo'. The derivation is clearly from dogs adopting such a posture. The phrase can be used figuratively to mean 'keep a low profile'.

fro   **[to and ...]**

Originating from Scottish and northern English dialects, and corrupted from the word 'from', the word 'fro' is most commonly in general usage in the phrase 'to and fro', suggestive of backwards-and-forwards movement but literally meaning 'towards and away'.

headlong   **[rush ...]**

The word 'headlong', which is descriptive of forward or downward motion, often at break-neck speed and usually with reference to the human body, with the head literally leading the way, can be used in various contexts but it is usually used in the phrase 'rush headlong' to emphasise the speed and lack of control of the motion in question. It can be used literally as well as figuratively. See also 'break-neck' under the adjectives section above.

hermetically   **[... sealed]**

The OED states that the word 'hermetically' is 'used to denote a method of sealing or closing a tube or vessel by fusing it at the opening, or by soldering or welding; hence, by any mode which renders it absolutely air-tight'. The word is only ever used in the phrase 'hermetically sealed'. It can also be found in the same phrase in the context of surgery.

muchly   **[ta ...]**

The word 'muchly' is mostly found in the colloquial phrase 'ta muchly', meaning 'thank you very much'. It can be used in other senses, but these are less common.

presto   **[hey ... !]**

'Presto' is a word used in music to describe the fast tempo of a piece. Outside of that context its use is most often confined to the phrase 'hey presto!', a command used by a magician to announce the climax of a conjuring trick.

scantily   **[... clad/dressed]**

'Scantily', meaning 'in a meagre or insufficient manner or measure', is usually used in the context of clothing, especially when referring slightly disparagingly to inadequately dressed young women.

soonest   **[least said ... mended]**

The word 'soonest' can occur as an adjective or an adverb. In both forms it literally means 'most soon', i.e. 'quickest', 'earliest' or 'speediest'. These words now tend to be used in its stead. It survives mainly in the proverb 'least said soonest mended', meaning 'the less said the better, as things will sort themselves out more quickly that way'. See also 'mended' in the verbs section above.

swimmingly   **[go ...]**

The word 'swimmingly', meaning 'with uninterrupted progress, such as when one is swimming', is almost always used with the verb 'to go', to signify smooth progress, as in such phrases as 'everything is going swimmingly' or 'it all went swimmingly, thank you'.

thither   **[hither and ...]**

Now largely superseded by 'there', the word 'thither' means 'towards that place'. It survives almost exclusively in the phrase 'hither and thither' (here and there) to mean 'to this place and that', often in the context of someone running around without apparent direction or purpose. The word 'hither' (here) is more commonly used on its own, including in such archaic phrases as 'come hither' (come here).

unawares   **[caught ...]**

Although the word 'unawares' can be used in several contexts, it is mostly commonly found in the phrase 'caught unawares', usually when describing someone who has been taken by surprise.

Prepositions

There do not appear to be any prepositions that are single-context words.

Interjections

An interjection is essentially an exclamation or an utterance that expresses emotion.

avast   **[… there, me hearties!]**

The word 'avast' is a nautical term derived from the Dutch for 'hold fast'. It means 'stop' or 'cease' and is usually followed in all its uses by an exclamation mark. It can be used without an object, but it is in most common usage in pirate movies in phrases such as 'avast there, me hearties!', i.e. 'stop what you are doing, fellow pirates!', often with an implication that further thought is necessary before continuing with the current action.

Conjunctions

According to the OED, a conjunction is 'an uninflected word used to connect clauses or sentences, or to coordinate words in the same clause'.

lest   **[… we forget]**

The word 'lest', meaning 'for fear that', is a rather archaic one. It can be used in more than one context, often in place of 'in case' or 'unless', e.g. 'he made sure she got home safely, lest any trouble befell her', but it tends to be used most in the stock phrase 'lest we forget' which accompanies war remembrance services and other commemorative occasions.

Lightning Source UK Ltd.
Milton Keynes UK
UKHW021100180920
370122UK00004B/68